two DATES a Week

REKINDLING THE SPARK

MARION OMALLEY
ART SCHERER

ISBN: 0615829422
ISBN 13: 9780615829425

CONTENTS

CHAPTER ONE
IS THIS BOOK FOR ME?

"You come to love not by finding the perfect person,

but by seeing an imperfect person perfectly."

—Sam Keen

IF

❖ You are in a committed love relationship, which has lost some or all of the "spark" it once had and

❖ You want to get that spark back, have more fun, and increase the long-term prospects of your partnership,

THEN …

Two Dates a Week, or TDAW, may just work for you!

+++++++++

"But how do I really know?" you ask.

Just keep asking yourself some of these questions and see where it leads you.

Truthfully now, answer the following:

Is time going too fast, and you just don't have enough of it for your relationship? Or does it sometimes feel so slow you know you're bored (a little or a lot), and sometimes wonder if you can revive "the patient?"

Does feeling truly happy and having fun together seem like a long shot these days, like love might be slipping through your fingers?

Is your couples' therapy lacking, and you're frankly wondering how much people can really change anyway?

Are you saying everything's "just fine," but you'd still like to relive some of the magic you once had and fall in love with life, and each other, again?

If any of these apply, the TDAW method can work for you!

We suggest you try TDAW for three months. It's simple. It's playful. It's effective. It's fun.

What Is a Committed Relationship?

By "committed relationship" we mean that two people have agreed to love and be loved by each other "till death do us part" (or some reasonable facsimile).

That's a tall order. Vows are not enough and they are not easy to keep. It takes courage and perseverance and humility and growth.

Along with being one of the hardest things to do in one's lifetime, it's also one of the best vehicles for true growth that life presents.

Whether you are married or unmarried, young or old, straight or gay, as long as you've got that someone special who has been by your side for a while, TDAW can help you anytime, but especially if your relationship is a little lackluster, and you want to juice it up!

4

Don't think you have to have a major problem to benefit, or, on the converse, that having a major problem will prevent TDAW from improving your life! It will improve your life.

Is "Losing the Spark" in a Long-term Relationship Inevitable?

We think so.

Perhaps there is one beatific couple somewhere on Earth who has never lost love for each other over the years. We have scoured our memories, though, and we cannot recall a single couple we've known over the last three decades who has not at some point, however briefly, thought, "I never saw THAT coming. How in the world did I ever choose to be with this _____?" (You fill in the blank.)

5

In long-term relationships there seems to be a common progression, or rather, a *regression* like the one pictured below:

❖ From initial attraction to mutual commitment.

❖ From commitment to "comfort" with each other and—this is key—comfort with the relationship.

❖ From comfort to taking each other for granted.

❖ From taking each other for granted to blaming each other for what's not right in the relationship or in your life in general.

Relationship Regression Spiral

ATTRACTION

COMMITMENT

COMFORT

TAKE FOR GRANTED

BLAMING

Added to the "regressive relationship" pattern described above are our own personal peccadilloes: skeletons in the closet, ego problems, power issues, and general "holes" in our own development, our own social/emotional health. When you think about it, it seems amazing that any couple can succeed in forging a juicy, long-term, committed relationship with all of this accumulated and often unconscious baggage.

Plus, once you've blamed your partner for what's not right in your life or your relationship, it's easy to make an enemy out of your (erstwhile) loved one, or certainly not to like them very much. At that point, it's also easy to go looking for love in all the wrong places, whether in the arms of another, addiction, work obsession, hobbies, porn, computer games, or television—or to give up altogether and become resigned to operating on parallel tracks.

How to Get the Spark Back

If you can relate to the dynamics of the above regression, but aren't ready to give up on your partnership, then TDAW could be the simple, no-blame plan for you. It just might right your re-lationship from nosedive to love hive. It will defi-nitely rekindle the spark.

Of course, "Into each life a little rain must fall." But if your relationship feels like it's got a semi-permanent dark cloud over it, it's time either to:

1. Get out of the relationship, or

2. Try something different in your current relationship.

We suggest the latter.

Note: TDAW is, of course, *not* a panacea for all the pitfalls couples face. Rather, it's a tool for keeping the relationship fresh, an antidote to creeping boredom, and an invitation to keep the spark alive through thick and thin.

It's often not about working harder on your relationship so much as about having more fun in it. Rather than complacency or complaining, TDAW is about seeing your relationship and your loved one through new eyes.

Try TDAW for three months. As we said before, it's simple. It's playful. It's fun.

Then please share your experience with us through the Feedback Form at www.twodatesaweekworks.com.

We want to know how it works for you!

CHAPTER TWO
HOW IT ALL STARTED

"Marriage is a romance in which the hero

dies in the first chapter."

—Unknown

For any two people to make a fun, interesting, sexy, and rewarding life together over time, effort is necessary.

We (Arthur and Marion) committed to the effort of building a life together. And though knowing we were two very different people from the start, we were, nonetheless, thrown for a loop by the force of our disagreements—many only minor-detail squabbles blown into full-fledged fights. Not to mention the bigger issues: money, time management, social life, and retirement. Back and forth we went.

Soon, the joy and the juice seemed to be bleached out of our entire relationship. Sex became pro-forma and infrequent. Real understanding flew out the window. We operated on parallel tracks.

We had fallen prey to the "relationship regression" mentioned in Chapter One. We blamed each other for the lack of love and intimacy, and we felt justified icing the other out or shouting back at the other's put-downs. We were both overly sensitive to the slightest raised eyebrow. (This from two individuals who knew about and taught caring communication and conflict resolution in our public and professional lives!)

Even if we didn't say it, what we thought most of the time was "you, you, you" (and not in a good way, like the old Ames Brothers' song.) Even on vacation, and especially on a trip when we were stuck in the car together, instead of seeing it as a long overdo opportunity to talk to each other, the slightest aggravation would set one of us off, unleashing a downward spiral that would spin out of control for hours, maybe even days.

If we were going to survive as a couple, we needed to do *something*. And somehow, we knew it was "to date"—to give ourselves a "time out" from the tiredness and turbulence, to meet each other in a new venue, and to behave differently with each other. We're not sure just how we got this idea. One of us thinks a therapist suggested it. The other remembers her parents' very good model of going out on dates frequently when she was a little girl.

Dating might rekindle our "good behaviors," we reasoned, which then, like good cells, would grow in number to overcome, or at least minimize, the bad cells. We might even like each other more, both during (and hopefully after) the dates.

To aid in this, one rule that quickly became a dating-behavior essential was that there would be *absolutely no discussion of problems on a date.* Slipping into the all-too-familiar recitation of our annoyances with life, work, and each other, or bringing up anything "touchy" and especially recriminations and blame, or someone's idea of how to fix it all, was not allowed.

Even if not on our best behavior all the time, we would at least be "good" twice a week, every week. We both now consider this a basic necessity even in ordinary circumstances if we want our life together to not only work, but to really sing! And now, most of the time it does!

A Whole New Life (Together)

It took us between one and two years to re-seed and nurture our relationship back into one of warm, wonderful love, and to rediscover real appreciation for each other. Imagine turning an aircraft carrier running at full speed completely around in the opposite direction. There is only one sure and safe way - bit by bit.

During that time we had to relearn how to invite each other out, plan for dates, and actually have fun and exciting times on our dates.

It was only after all three of our grown children, and several of our friends, asked us, "What's happening with you two? You seem so happy, so lovey-dovey?" that we realized what a turnaround we'd made. Sometimes our friends wondered out loud what had put the new spring in our step, or they commented that we seemed more in love ("What's with you guys?"), many having witnessed firsthand how "bickery" we could be over a minor detail in a story told at the dinner table. (We can still bicker with the best of them, but it doesn't stop the dating.)

As our relationship and love life started to improve, we began to enjoy each other more consistently, as well as to resolve (or at least manage) our conflicts. Simultaneously, we began to hear from friends and strangers alike about the "stuckness" or staleness of their own long-term relationships. We noticed this in old and young couples, in couples from different countries or the same hometown, in straight and gay partners, married or unmarried. Everywhere, lovers were suffering together, sometimes a little, sometimes a lot, sometimes quietly, sometimes not.

We talked about what had made the difference for us. And even now, when we start feeling bored or dissatisfied with each other, ourselves or our lives, what do we quickly resort to?

"Better do the dates!" one of us reminds the other. "We need to get back to TDAW!"

And so we do it. Date.

No analysis. No recriminations. Just the dates.

Simply put, the *Two Dates a Week* plan saved our marriage.

Now we have regular fun together. We appreciate each other. We learn while we're having fun. We touch more, give and receive more massages, and have better sex. We look forward to being together, on and off dates. We see that we really are, if not the vehicles for each other's dreams, the steady sidecar. We are very happy to be partners.

Sure, from time to time we still have issues— even some of the same ones. Not all conflicts can be resolved. Some can only be managed. But many of ours have simply melted away, or they don't seem as important now. As our daughter once said, "You can put up with a lot of crap when you've had a good date!"

Now, we want to help other couples drifting toward the same scary rocks that threatened us for so many years. Or who are just plain bored and know it could be better. Thus, we formalized the TDAW plan, and we wrote this how-to-do-it book.

TDAW supports us. Every week. Every year. Through all the thick and thin.

It can do the same for you.

Try it for ninety days. That's thirteen dates apiece—a sweet baker's dozen. Commit to it.

TDAW will revitalize your union. What have you got to lose?

With TDAW, we aim to create more love, peace, and creativity in this world, one couple at a time.

Go to our website: twodatesaweekworks.com

for FREE Updates and Ideas inside!

CHAPTER THREE
WHAT IS A DATE?

"Dating is a place to practice

how to relate to other people."

—Henry Cloud

It is difficult to have a meaningful discussion about dating without first understanding what we mean by going on a date.

A date is a time when two people get together to do something playful, pleasant or creative; they do something entertaining, or something that stretches them.

A date is a time to focus on each other and on the relationship.

Why? So you will like each other more and want to do it again. So you will learn more about each other and focus on the things you like about the other person.

Otherwise, we would call it a meeting, an encounter, or a transaction.

There are endless comments about this subject on eHOOKUP.com and other internet sites. Someone named KinkyJ, who manages that site, asks the following questions of her readers: Is it a date just to enjoy an activity that both parties profess an interest in, or must there be a potential for sex? More dates later? Marriage? Children?

One poster replied, "It's a commitment before commitment."

We would add to that last poster's comment that a date can also be a commitment *after* commitment!

To repeat, a date is two people getting together to have some fun and hopefully discover some-thing about each other and themselves.

Dates do not have to cost money, or be outside the home, or require a lot of energy! (Well, they do require some energy, and particularly of a certain kind, but not necessarily a lot, and they often give back far more than they take.)

A date can last an hour—or two or three or four. The intent is what's important. It is both the thought, the planning for a different kind of experience to please you and your mate, *and* the behavior on the date.

Twelve Characteristics of a Good Date

Five or more and you have a first-class date.

- ❖ Takes you out of the routine

- ❖ Is fun

- ❖ Is win-win

- ❖ Is kind and polite

- ❖ Sparks positive feelings

- ❖ Is relaxing and/or exciting

- ❖ Opens things up or opens you up

- ❖ Leads to loving looks

❖ May include gentle touching

❖ Ignites chemistry and brings back "that loving feeling"

❖ Doesn't break the bank (No economic regrets)

❖ Shows extra effort

Consider These Three Points

1. We all know about dating from our own experiences. And we've also all seen movies about dating, and heard things about others' good and bad dates.

2. We've also been on dates that didn't make it to the second date. So, if we think about it, we also know what *not* to do.

3. Then there were the dates where it didn't matter if we weren't a perfect match, because we were just enjoying the moments.

This, then, is what you are going to learn how to do again through TDAW: Enjoy (more of) the moments of your life together with the person to whom you once committed your "undying love."

What a Date is Not!

A date is *not* "You wanna' go out to dinner to-night and catch a movie?"

For too many years that's what we thought a date was. We'd find ourselves free of the kids for a night and decide to go out on the town. The problem was, as the old bumper sticker says, "Wherever you go, you take your head with you." So in our case, we took our non-dating mindsets out on the town with us.

We'd be sharing a lovely dinner with either nothing to talk about—while staring at the other couples in the restaurant and imagining their fantastic tête-à-têtes, cooing sweet nothings, unlike us—or we'd snipe about nonsense. Then we would see a film, drive home in silence, and crawl into separate corners of the bed.

A date for us now is an occasion to come together, and this is important: *it has been planned, in advance, by one or the other.* That doesn't mean we can't have spontaneous rendezvous, but the majority of our dates are planned and 'calendrated' ahead of time.

CHAPTER FOUR
RULES OF TDAW

"The life and love we create

is the life and love we live."

—Leo Buscaglia

Here are the Rules, or what we prefer to call our Agreements:

1. Take turns. Have two dates, one by you, one by your spouse or partner, every week that you possibly can!

Taking turns is a good thing. Both partners initiate, both accept. Both give, both receive. Both control or lead; both allow themselves to be controlled or led. As you learn to take turns initiating dates—and being the recipient of the other's largesse—it is our contention that you will learn to take turns initiating and receiving in other parts of your life too.

2. Plan your date on your own, ahead of time.

Don't talk about it too much in advance, especially not "What do you think about going to _____, honey?"

3. Be on your best date behavior—both of you.

And remember, if you weren't on date behavior early in your relationship, you wouldn't have gotten a second date. You *have* done it. You *can* do it again.

4. Pick up the tab on your date, unless you arrange in advance to divide the cost with your partner.

Do only what you can afford to do. Once again, fantastic dates do not have to cost much, or any, money!

5. Let your partner know what time to be ready, how to be dressed, and any other necessary info for the date. ("You'll need to eat beforehand," etc.)

6. Be on time with everything you need for an excellent date.

A date is not to be broken or missed except for emergencies. Don't be that jerk who is a no-show.

7. Let everything else go and have fun!

Helpful Hints

As the leader do the following:

- Brainstorm possible dates that you would like, or that he or she would like.

- Try new experiences. Ask yourself, "What is a date that neither of us would think of without expanding our horizons a little, or getting out of our comfort zones?"

- Scan the activities in your community paper and online, and note the interesting ones on your calendar prior to setting date nights (or days) with your partner for the coming week.

- Select a date that you want to do. In the final analysis, this is your date, and you get to select.

- Be flexible. The timing of a date is about when both of you can do it.

Don't do the following:

- Use your role as the "leader" as an opportunity to have your partner do things she or he is opposed to, or *really* dislikes or hates. (Although it does not have to be his or her favorite thing.)

- Choose activities you think would be "good" for her or him.

- Fall back on the same old kinds of dates you've always done (e.g., movies, dinner, sports, etc.) unless they are really fun and/or special for you both.

- Cancel the date at the last minute without very important exigencies. (Short of sickness or a family emergency or mutual agreement to cancel, the date is sacrosanct.)

As the follower, do the following:

- Be RAW (Ready, Able, and Willing).

R.A.W.
Ready, Able, and Willing

- Be open to new experiences and doing things your partner likes to do for this short period of time, even if you don't particularly enjoy it.

- Be appreciative of the planning and thought your partner put into the date, even if it's not your cup of tea.

- Be sweet and interested and polite—like you would be on a date!

- Put a smile on your face (even if you have to act). Remember: SMILE = Start My Internal Love Engine!

S.M.I.L.E
Start My Internal Love Engine

- Follow your date's lead!

Don't do the following:

- Be a no show.

- Be late.

- Complain about your date's choice of activity or make faces. (Watch your "nonverbals.")

- Be afraid or resistant to trying new experiences.

- Match your date dollar for dollar (i.e., how much they spend on their dates.)

- Relapse into discussions about anything problematic.

- Criticize.

- Have food in your teeth or smell bad.

CHAPTER FIVE
REMEMBERING HOW: DATING BEHAVIORS

"Marriage is not a noun; it's a verb. It isn't something you get. It's something you do. It's the way you love your partner every day."
—Barbara De Angelis

Equally important to following the rules of TDAW is that each partner agrees to come to each date with his or her best dating behavior on. By dating behavior we mean that each person will do the following:

❖ Get centered before the date.

❖ Focus only positive energy on their partner throughout the entire date.

Getting Centered *Before* the Date

It's less important *how* you do this than that you do it, especially if you and your mate have not been totally supportive of one another, or loving toward each other, in the days before the date.

To clear one's head, and get one's body and mind relaxed, yet focused, some people meditate for ten or fifteen minutes. Some listen to soothing music while taking a pre-date bath. Others might do stretching exercises or take a walk. (But don't just take that extra drink and call it 'getting centered.')

Any athlete at the top of her game will tell you that the most important minutes of the contest are those few right before the big game, when she visualizes her moves, the flow of the team, and the desired outcome. Any worthy job applicant gets himself ready before walking into the boss's office. See with some detail, and *feel* how you envision the date to go.

Aren't you worth it, and doesn't your partner deserve that little bit of focused effort to get your head, heart, and body in a relaxed, loving place prior to the date, whether you're the leader or the follower?

Focus Positive Energy on Your Partner Throughout the Date

Experts in human communication tell us that over 80 percent of what we put out and get back from others is in the form of *non-verbal* communication. Therefore, the facial expressions, the body language, the eye rolls, and the grunts and giggles of a given date are probably more important to how it feels to your partner than all the spoken words put together.

If non-verbal communication is the majority of what we transmit to each other, the most powerful asset we have in communicating is to be a good listener. Who has ever come home from work and complained about how much someone paid attention to her? "He just wouldn't stop listening!" is a gripe we seldom hear.

All good communicators know that listening is a prerequisite to being heard. What makes a good listener? Entire books are devoted to this, but here's our short list.

A good listener does the following:

- Turns one's body to the speaker.

- Looks at the speaker with warm and interested eyes.

- Doesn't interrupt.

- Gives subtle, non-verbal signals that he or she is listening (e.g., nods, says, "hmm hmm," smiles in recognition, etc..). These are called "minimal encouragers."

- Responds verbally and lets the speaker know that he or she has been heard, regardless of the listener's opinion on the subject, which may or may not be sought.

(Remember, *and this is important,* listening does not mean agreement!)

If you want to turn your partner on, think back to both the non-verbal and verbal communication you had on your earliest dates. Then on your next date, embody who you were with him or her way back when. If you listened a lot twenty years ago on the first three dates, listen a lot tonight. If you stroked his hand, or gently rubbed her neck while driving, try it again. That's the behavior of the person your partner fell in love with.

Both of us are old enough to know what science is discovering every year: Old dogs can learn new tricks. And remember their old ones too.

For the purposes of TDAW, it's comforting to realize that some of the new tricks or behaviors you need to learn to reignite your romance aren't "new" at all. They are simply forgotten ways of behaving that got the old dog that shares your bed today to fall in love with you all those years ago.

Dating Behaviors: What to Do!

- Send positive energy to your partner. Energy is real!

- Pay attention to your communication, non-verbal and verbal.

- Remember the old adages: *Pretty is as pretty does, attitude is half, love is an active verb*, etc. Be especially polite and as pleasing as you can be in the moment. Don't talk about your bad day, at least not right away.

- Talk only of neutral or positive things.

- Listen! Try not to interrupt.

- SMILE: Start My Internal Love Engine!

- Touch your partner.

- Look into your partner's eyes; see the soul of your partner.

- Choose curiosity. Be curious about every-thing said or done, not judgmental. Even non-verbally.

Non-dating Behaviors:

What *not* to Do!

- Ignore your date.

- Talk over your date (interrupt).

- Say little; seem distracted or bored.

- Act superior or be critical.

- Look too appreciatively at any or everyone else.

- Bring up past romances.

- Stand with your arms at your sides (never reaching out to your partner).

- Rush your date.

- Be impatient with your date.

- Let the door slam in your date's face.

- Make assumptions or put-downs.

Go to our website: twodatesaweekworks.com

for FREE Updates and Ideas inside!

CHAPTER SIX
TYPES OF DATES

"Love is friendship set on fire."

—Jeremy Taylor

Consider our date categories below merely as starting points for you to create and continually expand your own lists of dates.

Free Dates

This is a big category for us, even when we're "in the money," for reasons other than necessity. (For example, we like to save for big dates: travel, trips overseas, and other adventures.)

We've also discovered that the people who organize and who attend free events, which are often creative, charitable, artistic, inspiring, or community-building, are some of the most fun people to be around!

Some Free Date Examples:

<u>Art Openings</u>: These are often Friday night dates—a good way at the end of the workweek to let our hair down with some Brie and wine. We both fancy ourselves artistic, and we find inspiration in the creativity of others. Sometimes an opening will be the first part of a longer date night; sometimes it's enough in itself, and we go home to turn in early.

Outdoor Concerts: The Triangle region of NC is a magnet for musicians, and offers an abundance of concerts in traditional settings as well as "on the lawn." Food and drink is often allowed, and we set up a cozy blanket for two. Note: This kind of date also works well when we offer our *own* children a date opportunity, by taking their children for the evening. With our grandchildren in tow, we all sing and dance and listen and nosh, thoroughly enjoying each other's company.

Author Readings: These opportunities thrive all year long, and are a particularly good option in the depths of winter when outdoor activities decline. We love writers and readers, and almost always come home inspired!

<u>Get-Outdoors Dates</u>: Canoeing (try it in the moonlight!), biking, taking picnics, getting in paddle boats; or taking car rides in the country to that cute little town only thirty minutes away. (Have you ever played the "Left-Right" game, where in turn, each one gets to say 'left' or 'right' and you see parts of the world you've never frequented? Fun at any age!)

<u>Walking</u>: Anywhere! Go around the neighborhood, to the local ice cream shop, to a nature preserve, or to a protected area. Walks are great dates! And a fantastic opportunity to swing your arms with abandon, or endlessly hold hands!

At-Home Dates

Before initiating the TDAW process, we thought of a date as a night on the town. Our consumer-oriented culture encouraged us to think that way. And why not believe it? We needed to escape from our kids and all the parental duties. We even fabricated ways to farm the children out to grandparents and slumber parties—but often we felt too exhausted, and we stayed at home anyway. Just cuddling up together with a DVD felt wonderful, and it was sometimes all we could manage! Hence, the birth of the at-home- date. Later, when our nest emptied, all kinds of new and exciting possibilities for our dating life opened up.

Admittedly, at-home dates may be difficult for parents with young children unless the kids *are* "farmed out" or the date is planned for <u>after</u> their bedtime. You may not think so, but this is actually possible! How long does it take to share a bath together or scratch each other's backs? (Please check out "Dates for Tired Parents".)

Our Favorite At-home Dates

<u>Giving One Another Massages</u>: It can be on the fly, or the leader can go all out in the preparation with oils, candles, scents, and music. Just caring enough to get into the right head space to give a really great massage is a leap forward. The anticipation can be a lot of fun, just like in the old days of "new love."

Creative Projects Together: Your role as the leader might be getting the materials ready, covering the dining table, and mocking up a prototype of the project—a building design or craft, for example. Or your job might be initiating the brainstorm for discussing the outline of this book.

Cooking: Without children, create a great meal together. Or the initiator buys and brings home a special dinner. Planning matters!

Dancing: Put all those ballroom and tango lessons to use! Cuddle and sway to a romantic CD or do a little "Kitchen Jig," as our daughter used to request!

<u>Bathe Together</u>: Luxuriously…in a Jacuzzi, shower, or bathtub with oils and music, surrounded by candles. Wash each other's hair, scrub backs. Look at the stars.

<u>Garden as a Team</u>: We love gardening. If we stick to the dating rules, TDAW can enhance cooperation in all kinds of projects that we wouldn't otherwise think of as date material.

<u>Couch-Potato Cuddling</u>: The television can be a good dating vehicle, if it leads to positive interactions and feelings, but *not* if it only results in zoning out or falling asleep in fifteen minutes. (Though sleeping side by side in a different space can feel good!)

Hot Tip!

Maybe on a walk or in the hot tub, tell each other, "Wouldn't it be nice if…" stories. Build "air castles" one at a time, but without having to be practical or focused on "what is" now. Envision some aspect of your ideal futures, individually, or with each other. Play with it. What would you love, at least in this moment?

When building 'air castles,' it is very important not to point out the possible downsides of an idea or to critique. There is no need for agreement or disagreement, including holding the dreamer to something they 'imagineered.' This is an "air castle," after all. Remember: No repercussions for dreaming or envisioning.

Sexy Dates

Planned sex doesn't have to be boring. Think of it as planned spontaneity, or appointments to take a breath together and relax, to communicate in a different way and be open to affection, physical or emotional.

<u>Note</u>: And this is important. A sexy date does not require sex! You or your lover should never feel forced to do anything you're not in the mood for.

Still, don't neglect sexy dates, even if you currently have little or no physical attraction for each other, whatever the reasons are. Chemistry is its own thing and can be influenced by a variety of factors. It is amazing what can trigger it sometimes.

(Writing actually turns one of us on. And the other is almost constantly eager and ready.)

If you look back over the TDAW rules, you will see that the effort put into preparing for any date, and the trust that builds over time by going along with your partner's plans, contributes to a better date, whether a picnic or a roll in the hay.

So even if you have small children, don't neglect sexy dates! Get a sitter and think oils, outfits, lighting, special foods and drinks, videos, and toys—all night or a long morning in bed. Whatever turns you on. Whether at home, in a motel room, or in a broom closet, be as imaginative as your morals (and joints) permit!

Make-up Dates

Let's face it. We all goof up from time to time.

Remember the country-western wisdom, "We always hurt the one we love?" This is the time for the make-up date.

Back in the age of constant bickering, neither of us felt like apologizing and proposing a make-up date. Now, with fewer insensitivities and faux pas, and a little more "c'est la vie," it's easier for one of us to say, "Oops, I blew it. How about I take us out to dinner for a change of scenery, or open a bottle of wine and run you a bubble bath?"

Make-up dates don't have to be long or drawn-out *mea culpas*. They are more likely to be spur of the moment. They are designed to show the other person that you really want to make amends. (Psst! Vulnerability and acknowledging mistakes is sexy!)

Longer Dates

This category includes everything from an overnight date to a B&B weekend to an overseas trip to special, extended birthday and anniversary celebrations.

We all look at each other sometimes and admit, "The world is too much with us. We've been working too hard. Let's get outta' here."

For us in North Carolina, it's usually the beach or the mountains, depending on the season.

These kinds of dates can be good, even with (grand)kids, if there is thoughtful, organized planning, and if opportunities are designed in advance to escape from them every now and then. (P.S. Bring the grandparents or another couple who would love to watch your kids and give you a break for an evening.)

Dates Unplugged

Especially in this day and age, another date we like is the "unplug from the media and technology" date, either away or at home. Whether focusing on exercise, gardening, romance, projects like co-writing this book, painting, writing poetry, or even spring cleaning, we sometimes make it an *unplug* time.

Unplug dates are amazing! Just try them! We have currently given up television, and only watch what we want on the computer with an HDML cable. That can be plenty!

Important Note: TDAW is about cutting away from work! In general, *do not* make or take work calls when you are on a date! Turn your phone off. Or better yet, if you are out, leave the disruptive creature at home.

Gasho Dates

We learned the Gasho process at a silent re-
treat, where we were to remain quiet throughout
the entire four days. (It was hard for both of us.) If
we had to speak to each other or, for example, ask
the leaders for a particular knife in the kitchen, or
tell someone something, we were to put our hands
together in a prayer pose and whisper the word
"Gasho." Only when acknowledged with a nod
could we speak, and again, only in a whisper.

62

As busy and talkative people, we now love this kind of date!

Respect for our own and the other's silence goes a long way in calming down the "monkey brain" and enabling us to do different, but absorbing things in the presence of another. We feel renewed. We can simultaneously be there for ourselves and for somebody else.

A Gasho date is kind. It is giving. It helps us appreciate each other deeply. Too much noise, accessibility to the outside world, chit-chat, and cloying togetherness can breed anxiety and annoyance, if not contempt - all of which we need to minimize as much as possible. Constant input keeps us from getting to the things that are really important in our lives, and maybe even from knowing what they are!

Modern life is often too loud and too mediated. The Gasho date places our doorknobs on the inside, not the outside, where others can open it anytime they want to. Gasho dates create a space where we can decide for a given period of time exactly what we want to let in or let out. And that feels good. (We also like to incorporate Gasho into our unplugged-time.)

Note: In Buddhism, Gasho is the simple act of putting your hands together, with the palms facing each other and the hands extended slightly out in front of you. Gasho can be used when greeting or acknowledging a person of respect (*every* person), often accompanied with the phrase "Gasho" or "Namaste."

The meaning of Gasho is the following:

God is represented by the left hand, self by the right hand. When you join your hands together in Gasho, you create complete unity. There is respect, but without differentiation. On the surface it may seem contradictory, because Zen says you must abandon the self. But through Gasho you harmonize your being with the cosmic system, with others, and with God.

NOTE: Science shows that the position of your hands influences the brain. If you make a fist, you are aggressive, and the mind feels it. The mind and attitude change, depending on whether your arms are crossed or your hands are shoved in your pockets or behind your back while walking.

Try the Gasho pose now.

CHAPTER SEVEN
GREAT DATES: WHERE AND HOW TO FIND THEM

"Dating is like searching for the perfect wine. One date is too fruity, another too dry, and still another too much bouquet (cologne overdose). But once you find the perfect variety that suits your taste, get drunk."

—Katie Kosko

The big events in a relationship (e.g., having children, losing parents, etc.) cause us to become deeper, both as individuals and as a couple.

Weekly dates are an opportunity to broaden, as individuals and as a couple. To expand.

Before we hit on TDAW, we trudged through all the familiar and well-worn ruts of long-term couples:

- Rarely dating (laziness, taking each other and our relationship for granted).

- Calling dinner and a movie a "date" more often than not (lack of creativity).

- Arguing about what to do on "tonight's date" or being decidedly unenthusiastic (conflict).

- Putting little thought into the date because he or she was likely to veto the plan any-way, or expecting the worst, or at least not the best, to happen, and then consequent-ly, in the end, causing that very outcome.

Now, with the TDAW plan, we know that each of us is responsible for one date a week, and we each have a routine.

Art looks forward every Wednesday to laying his hands on a copy of *The Indy,* our area's best weekly source for sniffing out new, creative, tasty, free, or fun dates.

He skims the entire paper, noting on the front page any good date possibilities (e.g., "p.38, Th., 7 pm, outdoor dance"), as well as any articles he wants to read later. If he gets distracted reading the articles, though, he often discovers, too late on Friday or Saturday, that he missed out on a really good date. For example, Marion's favorite author gave a reading of her latest work, with a live band, *last* night!

Gleaning *The Indy* is now one of his favorite weekly rituals. It also primes the dating pump, keeping him alert to dating opportunities all week long, wherever they might present themselves. (as well as to activities he wants to do by himself when Marion is out of town or uninterested.)

Marion's method is to seize on the "available" night first and then make a Plan A date and a Plan B date. Plan A might be an at-home date, and intentionally low-key, in case one (or both) is unexpectedly drained. Plan B is a date out, frugal or extravagant, depending on whether or not her boat—i.e., the USS Paycheck—came in.

Have you experienced the phenomenon where you are oblivious to your surroundings until you give them your attention? For example, you never see any green VW Bugs on the road until you buy one, and then, "Poof," there they are, zooming around everywhere.

And so it is with good dates. Once you make the initial effort to start planning, they crop up all over the place!

You're getting a cone at the local ice cream shop. Waiting in line, you hear the woman in front of you talking on her cell phone about the Dalai Lama giving a talk titled, "Humor and Compassion: The Clown's Road to Enlightenment" this Friday night! After she finishes the call, you learn she is one of the organizers, and you walk out of the shop with a double-chocolate sugar cone and two compli-mentary front-row seats to see the Dalai Lama (or maybe some lesser-known luminary...but you get the idea.)

If you and/or yours are literary types, scan the boards at the public library or bookstores for up-coming events, and the universe will start bending your way.

With the internet, none of us have excuses any-more! Not to mention GroupOn, LivingSocial, or OurLocalDeal, which often offer huge discounts on dates. (Our daughter got a two-day weekend at a romantic inn in Pittsboro with breakfast for one hundred dollars!)

You're the sporting or outdoor type? (Or would like to be?) Then get on the email list of your local REI or parks and recreation department. Embarking on a new adventure with the one you love, like rock climbing, biking, whitewater rafting, or hot-air ballooning, often makes for a fabulous date!

Good dating is like good reading or good sex: you never run out of new possibilities. The more you do it, the better you get, and the more your entire world will expand.

CHAPTER EIGHT
DATES FOR TIRED PARENTS

A baby changes your dinner party conversation

from politics to poops.

—Maurice Johnston

There's no such thing as a parent who hasn't been really, really, tired.

Whether it's an infant who's been up for hours at night, or dealing with a sick five year old, or your job, or keeping up with the chores and the yard, and each other, from time to time, all parents are plumb exhausted. Sometimes, it feels like a semi-permanent state of mind (and body).

Exhaustion can throw a monkey wrench into the best plans to have good date times with your partner. Therefore, tired reader, we offer a few suggestions for keeping your date-lives alive during those exhausted periods.

JUST CALL ANY AND ALL OF THESE THINGS A DATE!

This one simple "reframing" will make all the difference! It's the thought that counts, the intention, even the wish ... and then the "date behavior."

1. Farm your kids out to the grandparents or a friend you trust. Get in bed and cuddle. Fall asleep together.

2. Ask her to come home after work and be ready for you to take care of everything. Do the shopping, prepare the bathtub, get the massage oil out and the candles and the soft music.

3. Fix her a good dinner. It doesn't have to be fancy. Light a few candles. Put out the placemats. At the end, rub her shoulders. Go to bed. Expect nothing, but be open to appreciation in the myriad ways it may show itself.

4. If you're really tired and you have a little tender in your pocket, get him a massage. You don't need to do it yourself. Just tell him you love him, and that this is a date.

5. Kiss for at least 1 minute without stopping (like you used to).

6. Play a game together. Make one up or play anything from "I Spy" to "Truth or Dare." Or "If

I could have one thing, be one place, or do one thing this year, it would be …."

7. Go on a scenic drive together with no particular destination.

8. Discuss a topic that is of interest to your spouse. Listen to him or her.

Here are some:

Three things about my marriage that I like very much:

Three specific things I personally could do to improve our relationship:

9. Rent a classic romantic move like *Casablanca. Sense and Sensibility, The Princess Bride, When Harry Met Sally, Notting Hill,* etc. For more movie ideas go to:

www.theromantic.com/romanticmovies.htm

10. Sit up in bed together for an evening of reading. Find a book you both enjoy and take turns reading to each other, or each of you can just read your own book side by side in each other's company. Maybe even a little 'footsy.'

11. Try star-gazing in your own back yard or out in the country. Go outside. Just bring a blanket for warmth or to lie on and gaze upwards together. If you're the scientific type, you might get a star map

and try to identify constellations, but that's not the main point.

12. After you put your children to bed, go downstairs, pour yourself a cocktail or a spritzer, and watch something you both like on TV or the internet together - just decompress. (But don't overdo the drinking or drugs.)

You get the idea. "Tired" might mean you don't have as much time or energy for your beloved. BUT ... it doesn't mean you can't give her or him one really good date a week!

CHAPTER NINE
COMMON MISTAKES COUPLES MAKE (AND HOW TO AVOID THEM)

"Unless you lovingly and energetically nurture your marriage, you will begin to drift away from your mate."

—Dennis Rainey

The biggest mistake is to assume, upfront, that the TDAW method will never work for you. If you don't try something new, you won't get something new. Ask yourself, "Do I really want to settle for either tired resignation or a split up?" Plato knew that "you can discover more about a person in an hour of play, than in a year of conversation." Especially the kinds of conversations we often have outside of a date.

Another mistake is to try dating once or twice... and then quit, either from falling back into ruts, or because the first attempts weren't so hot. Remember, we are asking only for a three-month commitment. New habits need a little time and practice to take, *but they're worth it!*

Dating is like using the treadmill. If you don't do it routinely, you might as well not do it at all, because once or twice doesn't get the change you're after.

A third mistake is to go on the date and then break all the rules by demonstrating anything but date behavior. You remember how you once were on a date, don't you? Even when you didn't especially like the person, you were polite. You were on your best behavior. Your "better angels" were in charge.

Do that now.

Another mistake is to present TDAW to your partner in a blaming or demanding way. Instead, lift both your spirits. Use your best communication skills and act as though you are really asking your partner on a date for the first time. Or use subterfuge. See Chapter Fourteen: "The Woman's Underground Guide to Two Dates A Week."

Don't let him or her throw you into a negative tailspin. Don't react; respond. Get that date with the person you love.

It's also helpful to remember that being a tit-for-tat person in a relationship never works! If you want your relationship to change for the better, then, as Gandhi put it, you have to be the change you want to see. As Gandhi even said, "I first learned the concepts of non-violence in my marriage."

And that means you have to model, model, model.

You do it first.

CHAPTER TEN
ELIMINATING EXCUSES

"Success is a tale of obstacles overcome, and for

every obstacle overcome,

an excuse not used."

—Robert Brault

We've written down some of the excuses from our kids and other couples about why TDAW is "Impossible!" for them to even consider. We've also tried to predict some of the excuses you might use to fink out on reenergizing your dating life. The excuses we came up with are in CAPITAL LETTERS. Our answers are in lower case.

WITH TWO YOUNG KIDS (OR TWO HIGH-POWERED JOBS, ETC.), WE DON'T HAVE TIME TO DATE.

Bo-o-o-o-o-gus. One of the best things you can do for your kids is to stoke the love relationship with their other parent. Like the old saying goes, "If Momma ain't happy, ain't nobody happy." And in 2013, we would add "Daddy" to that adage. Remember, children pick up your energy, good, bad, and otherwise!

It's similar to saying you don't have time to exercise. You can get away with that for awhile, especially when you're young, but eventually every healthy person realizes that regular exercise gives us more alert time and more energy, allowing us to be more productive, healthy, and happy, which improves all aspects of our lives.

The same is true with dating. Life is far more than surviving or making money. Or even being a parent. Life is an occasion. Make it special! Twice a week!

OK, SO WHO'S GONNA TAKE CARE OF THE KIDS WHEN WE'RE OUT ON A DATE?

Again, unless you live on a deserted island, bogus. Possible places to find baby sitters include your neighbors and CraigsList (Insist on three references). Ask around at your local house of faith, day care center, or high school for mature teenagers who are good sitters. Or since parents of young children tend to hang out with other parents of young children, form or join babysitting co-ops that trade off so each couple gets to date each and every week.

And don't say your children won't like the sitter. How do you know? Your children need to like people other than you, and they need to learn to engage respectfully with people who are not their favorites too. This helps them their whole life!

I/WE LIKE THE IDEA OF DATING, BUT TWO PER WEEK SOUNDS LIKE WORK, AND IT'S JUST NOT POSSIBLE.

OK, we'll cut you a little slack here at the onset, as long as you promise to go on at least one date every week, and you promise to take turns in leading each date.

If you do so, we believe that once you get in the *habit* of dating again, you'll start looking forward to it so much that you will make the time for two dates a week. The analogy to regular exercise comes to mind again: The first week or two after a long hiatus is tough. But by the third or fourth week, you can't wait to get home and ride the bike or grab your racket and head for the tennis court with your partner.

WHO'S GOT MONEY FOR DATING?

Remember those free dates we discussed in Chapter Six? Or get a cookie jar for your spare change at the end of the day. Also, anytime either one of you says an unkind word to the other, you can drop a buck in the "dating jar." Then, whenever you go out on a date that's not free, add the contents of the jar to whatever you've got in your wallet. Your relationship is worth investing in. Period.

YOU WANT ME TO DATE THAT OLD GOAT (HAG) WHO I CAN HARDLY STAND OR BORES ME TO DEATH?

Look, our thoughts are either get out of the relationship or get back in with both feet. In our own experience, had we gotten on the TDAW plan years earlier, the only thing we would have missed out on was a lot of suffering.

Unless you and your partner are pathological sadists, you fell in love with each other, in part, because you thought you could be happier with each other than without each other. Just because the last few days, weeks, months, or even years have been routine and boring, or conflict-laden, doesn't mean you can't rekindle the old flame.

But you've got to make the effort. You've got to suspend your disbelief, even if only during the date at the outset. (We'll discuss this more fully in Chapter Eleven.)

In Norman Doidge's fabulous book <u>The Brain that Changes Itself</u>, he points out that there is a chemistry to both the pleasures and pains of love, and one of the "happy" chemicals is dopamine. Dopamine likes novelty. When monogamous couples develop a tolerance for each other and lose the romantic high they once had, "this may not be a sign that either of them is inadequate or boring, but that their plastic brains have so well adapted to each other that it's harder for them to get the same buzz they once got from each other."

What to do? Doidge goes on to say, "Fortunately, lovers can stimulate their dopamine, keeping the high alive, by injecting novelty into their relationship. When a couple go on a romantic vacation or try new activities together, or wear new kinds of clothing, or surprise each other, they are using novelty to turn on the pleasure centers, so that everything they experience, *including each other*, excites and pleases them. Once the pleasure centers are turned on and globalization begins, the new image of the beloved again becomes associated with unexpected pleasures and is plastically wired into the brain, which has evolved to respond to novelty."

In life, we've found, you've got to control your thoughts, or your thoughts will control you. And your actions.

If you make the commitment to try TDAW for three months, and simultaneously, jot a note in your calendar ninety days hence to reflect on how your feelings toward your partner have changed, we are betting on you and yours to grow and change for the better, and to be one helluva' lot happier together. And your actions.

NOW THAT THE SHEEN OF "NEW LOVE" HAS WORN OFF, WE FIND THAT WE'RE JUST INTERESTED IN DIFFERENT THINGS.

That's even more reason to get together and date!

As we mentioned earlier, back before we codified the TDAW plan for ourselves and learned to take turns planning the dates, we often disagreed about what we were going to do on the date, and by the time we went out, we either resented each other or were lackadaisical about the experience.

Now that we share the leadership of the dates, each week, we find ourselves discovering a much more diverse life together. Sometimes I plan a date for her/him that I think s/he would really like; sometimes I plan a date that I know I'll really like and I suspect s/he will too.

The thing that's missing--THANK GOD--is arguing about what date we're going to go on: tonight, tomorrow, or later this week. We are each in charge. We each hit home runs from time to time. And we each occasionally strike out. But that's ok, because now, we're on the same team, and win or lose, we get to go home together....

CHAPTER ELEVEN
LIVING WITH
DIFFERENCES

"The ultimate test of a relationship is to disagree

but to hold hands."

—Alexandra Penney

By now, we guess that you no longer expect your partner to fulfill all of your dreams, and that you are probably somewhere in the inevitable power struggle, or have been there and now have settled, though you may still be struggling to accept each other's differences.

wherever you are, good partnerships and marriages can be built between two people with very different *modus operandi* and values. And, hello! Don't they need to be built between different kinds of people all over the world?

Of course, the so-called little things, the daily habits and preferences—what we like to call differences with a "little d"—can drive you crazy. We know:

Morning Dove vs. Night Owl; Neat vs. Messy; Visual vs. Kinesthetic; Punctual vs. Late; Talkative vs. Quiet; Indoors vs. Outdoors; Fussy vs. Laidback. You get the picture.

Now ask yourself, "Are any of these 'little d's' truly worth ending my relationship?"

Of course, you can spend your whole life fighting about them. And many people, including us, do!

Until we don't.

A lot of people choose being right over being happy—or try to lay claim to it anyway.

But differences, even the big ones, are not a reason not to date. They are the reason *to date*. Our world demands it. Our relationships demand it. If we are to grow and evolve, we need to water the damn plants! Prepare the soil. Pull out the choking weeds. Get a little sunlight.

We don't need to talk about our differences all the time. Or icily *not* talk about them. We don't need to judge and bristle every minute of the day! Or decide to just not care.

Rather, we can look at each other for a few hours with curiosity, not judgment. With love.

We can be quiet about our differences. It won't kill us. It may rekindle something and put freshness back into a relationship that seems way past its shelf life!

Get with the program, this program. Try it! Dating.

TDAW is not a substitute for counseling, but it is a kind of therapy, a healing process, in itself. Remember, life is too short to rely eternally on the therapist's couch. TDAW works!

CHAPTER TWELVE
HOW TO DATE THE MATE YOU "HATE"

"What counts in making a happy marriage is not so much how compatible you are, but how you deal with incompatibility."

—Leo Tolstoy

We've put the word "hate" in quotation marks for a purpose. By the above rhyming title we really mean, "How to date the mate whose behavior, or lack thereof, towards you, you hate." (See why we didn't use that clunky title?)

If you really hate your partner, have a white-hot, searing hatred for his or her very soul, you may need to seek counseling or legal advice rather than dating advice. If that is not the case, though, then let's proceed.

Our Beliefs:

- It's easier to get out of shape than it is to stay in shape.
- It's easier to make a mess than to clean it up.
- It's easier to fall in love than to stay in love.
- It's easier to blame the other than to change myself.
- Things we value (including relationships) are worth working for.

- And, most importantly, the only person I can change—and it ain't easy—**is** *myself.*

Thus, if you're having a hard time liking the person you're going on a date with, we suggest the following:

Suspend your disbelief.

And then ask yourself, "What might he or she dislike about me?" Then change *that* behavior (or behaviors).

Suspending Your Disbelief

We all know how this technique works in our enjoyment of books or movies. In order to enjoy *Harry Potter*, we have to suspend our disbelief about boys and girls being able to fly on brooms during a quiditch match. In order to enjoy *The Wizard of Oz,* we have to suspend our disbelief about scarecrows and tin men and lions being able to talk and comfort Dorothy.

With TDAW, we're turning this technique on its head. Instead of believing that the "magical" things your partner is doing are real, "magically" rearrange your head and believe that the grouch you live with can be charming on tonight's date, or that the cold, hard, distant creature you share a life with can be warm and expansive. (Or at the very least, that *you* can.)

Envisioning means that you see what you want it to be. Expectations matter (particularly as long as we don't *insist* on them.) We tend to get out of life what we expect we will get out of life. And focus on.

Intention. Attention. Focus.

The same can be said about dates.

So doctor, examine thyself. If you've been expecting more crap and put-downs, or cold, blank, disinterested stares from your partner, maybe your next date is your opportunity to envision wonderful things, affirmations, and loving looks from your main squeeze.

Along with changing your expectations, we suggest that you use dates to change your (own) actions. Our favorite technique in this area is called "acting as if."

Ask yourself, "If he were loving, supportive, attentive, caring, funny, and sexy, how then would I act in response?" Then, behave toward her or him that way, as if it were as natural as breathing. You are in control. Don't get trapped by the "What-Is-Ness" you see and hear around you! Keep your eyes on the prize. *Cultivate the vision.*

Don't do this for any particular result. Don't do it to feel superior in the relationship. Don't just do it once or twice and then give up when nothing changes in how you are being treated. Act "as if" without motive, for your own growth, so that you will feel better, happier. Do it in a playful way (like you're in a show that you wrote). Do it as a long-term experiment.

If you suspend your disbelief (about how terrible, boring, butt-headed, stodgy, and so on your partner is), and if you act "as if" your partner is already the dream boy or girl you imagine, one of two things will happen:

EITHER

1. As you lighten up and become more loving and supportive on your dates, your partner will start imitating your positivity, and before long that good feeling will start creeping into your phone conversations, the kitchen, the sofa, the bedroom....

OR

2. In spite of your best efforts, your partner, over the long haul, will refuse to budge an inch. Then, even if your relationship is headed to ruin, you'll

have the consolation of knowing that you were your loving best over the months or years before you both decided to call it quits.

Remember, for many, if not for most of us, dating was difficult when we tried it the first time, and not always fun at all. When we got married, we were glad we didn't *have* to date anymore.

But for some of us at least, as we grew and developed, dating became easier and easier. And for those who finally found that special someone, it turned into a beautiful dance, a night on the town, pure bliss. As Paul Simon sang, "There were days of miracles and wonder."

If you're asking yourself, "Then why has dating become so difficult for us?" we suggest that you forget the "whys" and focus on the "hows," the hows of getting your date life back on track. Not by changing anything about your partner, but by changing first your *inner* approach to dating, and then changing your *outer* behavior to your partner, first on the dates, and then, one by one, in all the other areas of your life and relationship together. Be a little kinder than necessary. Do something different.

It's not magic, but it just might feel like it.

Go to our website: twodatesaweekworks.com for FREE Updates and Ideas inside!

CHAPTER THIRTEEN
HOW DO I PRESENT TDAW TO MY PARTNER?

"Most broken hearts are caused by

unspoken words."

—Unknown

If you haven't been dating for a while, or have been breaking all the Dating Rules on your dates, it's important to take care and be strategic in how you initiate your "new" dates with your partner. Here are some possible scripts.

Script Number One

"John, I would like for us to start dating each other again."

"Why?"

"So we can remember and appreciate our love relationship again, separate from the business, parenting, and daily-living part of our relationship."

"That sounds silly. Who has time for dates? Or money?"

"We do. And frankly I'm not sure we have time *not* to date again. Let me take you on the first date. Then you take me on one."

"What do you mean, 'We don't have time *not* to date'? And we don't have a sitter."

"We can get one. I'll handle the first date. Would you go out with me next Thursday night?"

112

"I have a meeting."

"Okay, I'm flexible. Which night is good for you?"

"I don't know. Maybe Saturday."

"Saturday it is. Please be ready at seven o'clock and just wear casual clothes."

"All right. What are we doing?"

"It's a surprise. And John, would you please read this list of dating do's and don'ts for me?" (You might want to copy them out of the book rather than placing the entire book in your partner's hands.) "I'm afraid we may have forgotten how to date, and I'd like our first date to be a really good one."

"What? You mean this is some scheme of yours?"

"Just read it...please. It'll take less than two minutes. And after you do, can I ask if you would agree to bring these behaviors to our date? I will too. I think it would help us."

"I guess so."

"Great! I am really looking forward to dating again, John."

(Kiss)

Script Number Two

"Mary, I think we need to go out on a date."

"Why? I don't have time. I'm too busy and tired. And we don't have the money, John!"

"Let me take you out! I'll choose something relaxing."

"I don't know. I just don't see..."

"Okay, I'll arrange a date at home then, just a couple of hours. You've got a couple of hours, don't you?"

"I don't know, John. Why do we need to date? What's the matter? What do you really want?"

"Nothing's the matter. I just want us to date. That's all. Like we did when we first fell in love. It could start with a back rub."

"And lead to what? I'm too exhausted for sex."

"Who's talking about sex? Let's take a walk, hold hands, and then I'll give you a backrub."

"That sounds nice."

"Seven o'clock? Tomorrow night? After dinner?"

"I don't even know what we're having for dinner."

"I'll bring home your favorite pizza. You don't have to do anything."

"Okay."

(Smile)

In these scenarios, you can decide when, where, or if to give him or her a copy of TDAW.

Ideally, you should *both* read it!

But it's not necessary!

HOWEVER, before proceeding, also read the next chapter: "The Woman's Underground Guide To Two Dates A Week."

CHAPTER FOURTEEN
THE WOMAN'S UNDERGROUND GUIDE TO TWO DATES A WEEK

"Fake it 'til you make it."

Unknown

We, the two co-authors of this book, one female and one male, wholeheartedly agree that it's likely the vast majority of people who pick up, page through, and buy this book will be women.

It's not that men don't want more fun, or juiciness, or (look out: here's a word we don't use too often in our gender) "connection" with the one we love.

It's just that many men have given up on dating as an avenue to that fun, juiciness, and connection. We often just want to sit around and then hit a home run: make out and make love.

Books could be written on why that is. This is not one of those books.

For our purposes: to bring more joy and fun and that old "spark" back into your committed relationship, let us suggest the following:

If you are the one who believes in the goals of this book, but are stuck with the one who will never "get with the program" as written, particularly if it is presented as a program, don't despair. Here are our tips.

1. Don't even mention that you've seen, paged through, or, especially, purchased this book.

2. As soon as you get home, hide it.

3. Read it only when he or she is away.

4. Return it to its safe hiding place each time you've finished with it.

5. Start slow. Ask him out on a date (or her), but, henceforth, we'll skip the "or her."

6. Repeat next week.

7. Repeat next week. The number of times this will need to be repeated depends on far too many variables to complete the numerical sequencing, but here are a few: Are YOU enjoying the dates? Is HE enjoying the dates? Is there any change in your daily interactions? More touching? Warm looks? Less sniping, etc.?

8. Repeat #6 and #7 until he asks you out on a date ... OR you suggest sweetly (if you can) or pointedly, if you must, that he take you out on a date next time (at which point you can carefully feed him a few of the rules...er, that's why we call them Agreements).

OR you give up and head for California.

Okay, we're being a bit glib, and we know we're not giving our due to gay couples or those unusual couples where the guy is the romantic and the girl is the bore, drudge, hopeless depressive, OCD, etc. Still, with over 125 years of life-experience between the two of us, we have seen certain patterns in the way women and men perceive dating and relationship rescue, in general, ESPECIALLY after said woman and said man have spent 10 to 20 or more years together. "What's wrong with our relationship the way it is?" you're likely to hear.

So be subtle. Be strategic. Dating is not only an activity, it is an attitude: a different way of being together, a break in the action. Do it. However you can. Fake it 'til you make it.

Date.

CHAPTER FIFTEEN
KEEPING EXPECTATIONS REAL

"Perseverance pays."

—The I-Ching

This is essentially a caveat, dear reader, to not expect great results *immediately* from your partner or yourself as you begin the TDAW plan.

You two probably didn't lose the spark in a few short weeks, and you're not likely to go from boredom or inactivity or downright hostility in your relationship to "Whoopee!" in a fortnight either.

But do remember, you don't even need to like your partner initially to be successful with TDAW. You just need to want to have more fun and more life in your relationship. That's all.

Again, plan to play with TDAW for at least three months. Make it a regular commitment before you give up on it. Play with it, and we do mean "play." Enter into your dating experiments with the same attitude a young child takes as she builds sandcastles at the edge of the ocean. Before long, the rising tide washes away every castle, but the fun is in the experience, and good or bad, there's always a new castle to build another day.

Whether you're the leader or the follower on a date, be open to it succeeding wonderfully. If it doesn't, if you wind up icing each other out in spite of your best intentions, or slip into annoying "no-no" topics, don't hold on to the bad feelings. Let them go. Watch the sandcastle be washed away, and promise yourself you'll be open to a great date next time, when you will remind yourself and each other of the dating rules and commit to following them.

Of course, it's understandable that after we've been hurt or disappointed so many times by our partner (and vice versa), we'd both be wary of having any great expectations for a given date. But unless we learn to open our hearts again, to act "as if," to play with the idea that we can bring this tired old relationship back from the brink, or enliven a good but stale one, what's the chance that anything's really going to get better?

Two Dates A Week

Resignation or holding a grudge is not part of the plan. It is not a prescription for getting the love light burning. TDAW *is* a prescription. Put it in your medicine chest!

Think of this: There is usually a profound difference in the time it takes most young children to get over a verbal or even physical conflict, and the much longer time it takes adults to do the same.

Why is that? Are those three- and four-year-old children smarter than us? More advanced spiritually? Or are they simply less committed to being right, to being the victim, to being the student or the teacher in a conflict? More ready to reconsider and play again? That's all you need to do.

Spiritual teachers exhort us to think of these people who bother us most, who get the deepest under our skin (in an *itchy* way), as some of *our* greatest teachers. See your partner in that perspective, *especially* when she or he is driving you mad. And then, with a few short breaths, realize that no one can drive us mad (or any other emotion) without our consent and active participation.

Okay. Let us use a few amazing figures for examples.

Remember when Jesus urged his followers to "Love your enemies." It was not with the notion that this would quickly change those enemies into warm and fuzzy friends. Rather, learning to love even *those* "blankety-blanks," was to grow in patience, perspective, and humility. That's what we'll be doing here, and that's not half bad!

And then there's Martin Luther King. Knowing that he, and the other foot soldiers of the early civil rights struggles, could not possibly match the dogs and the water hoses, or the guns of the police and others opposed to them, he urged his followers to respond to violence with *love*. (By the way, Dr. King is on record as saying that he had no illusions that love would instantaneously change the hardened hearts of the deliverers of violence, but *over the long haul*, responding to those hard hearts with love was the best, if not only, successful strategy open to them.)

If this is true on the macro level, it certainly is true on the micro level for us in our twosomes.

Beat the odds.

Just because it is simple, doesn't mean the TDAW plan is simpleminded.

"Coming from ultimate love helps us to go into the area of romantic love."

—Bill Bowen

CHAPTER SIXTEEN
AND FINALLY, THERE'S YOU, THERE'S ME, THERE'S US

"Love doesn't make the world go round. Love is what makes the ride worthwhile."

—Elizabeth Browning

There's you. There's me. There's us.

Sometimes, life with your partner is like an easy game of catch: one ball, two gloves, equal joy in the throw and return. The ball, of course, is the relationship.

Certainly, there are plenty of times when there is little or no squabbling or dissent, when there is peace and deep caring between the two of you. When together, it feels like you are creating something beautiful.

So maybe the *Two Dates a Week* plan is not always a matter of "saving" your relationship, but rather, of revitalizing it, just making it sing again!

It's easy to fall in love. But it's also easy to fall into a rut with the one you love. Romantic love can be fleeting. In today's 24/7-world, we often don't make the time to care for our relationships. And we are all creatures of habit. The quotidian, our daily life, is powerful!

TDAW encourages you to make dating a habit again.

TDAW is a "process-design solution," a way to routinely add something positive to your relationship that can be foundational in countless other areas of your life. As mentioned before, it is worth repeating the wisdom of our daughter: "You can put up with a lot of crap when you've had a good date!"

And it's true! It is our belief that this book will bring a lot more fun to couples' lives! And, for us, that's a goal worth pursuing.

Experiment with TDAW, and take having fun seriously too. We try to wake up each morning with the following affirmation: "Today I will help somebody, I will make some money and I will have some fun."

Make a commitment to yourself and to your partner. What do you have to lose? Nothing, really, but your tired, old habits.

Marion's mother used to say, "Marriage is a hard school." And for sure, loving together over a lifetime takes effort.

But as hard as long-term partnerships can be, they don't have to be *so* hard! They can also be fun, a source of expansion, of delight, of renewal, even inspiration!

A spiritual path.

Dating.

We know what making it a habit did for us—and still does! We know what it can do for you too.

Two dates a week!

Let's make it a movement!

CHAPTER SEVENTEEN
RESOURCES

"Some pray to marry the man they love. My prayer will vary. I humbly pray to heaven above that I love the man I marry."

—Rose Pastor Stokes

TDAW is not individual or couple's therapy, and it does not solve all relationship problems. It does not get your partner to change, get over past hurts, interrupt an affair, avoid a separation, teach you how to forgive and be forgiven, or provide a thousand other marriage-crisis solutions. In short, it does not focus on the problem. It helps us remember to focus on and practice the positive, the solution, or at least one of them – dating and treating each other as if we were both 'precious.' And in doing so, changes for the better cannot help but fall into place.

For us, when we practice the plan faithfully, TDAW is no less than transformative.

The energy of an answer is always different from that of the question. It was dating that took us to that new energy!

The following books have helped us. Please email other recommendations you'd like us to consider for the second edition of *Two Dates a Week*, soon on its way. We would love to have them!

www.twodatesaweekworks.com

Happy trails, and keep on dating!

A New Earth: Awakening to Your Life's Purpose by Eckhart Tolle

Be Here Now by Ram Dass

Be the Person You Want to Find: Relationship and Self Discovery by Cheri Huber and June Shiver

Emotional Intelligence: Why It Can Matter More Than Intelligence by Daniel Goleman

Fun and Creative Dates for Married Couples: 52 Ways to Enjoy Life Together by Howard Books

Getting the Love You Want: A Guide for Couples by Harville Hendrix

Mars and Venus Together Forever: Relationship Skills for Lasting Love by John Gray

Men Are from Mars, Women Are from Venus by John Gray

Peace Is Every Step by Thich Nhat Han

Pucker Up by Tristan Taormino

Social Intelligence: The New Science of Human Relationships by Daniel Goleman

The Brain that Changes Itself by Norman Doidge, M.D.

The Law of Attraction by Abraham Hicks

CHAPTER EIGHTEEN
DATE PLANNING FORM

"Planning prevents piss-poor performance."

Unknown

1) Leader:_____

   Our next date:_____

   Day of the week:_____

   Time of the date:_____

2) Are there any special events or good dates
   presenting themselves at this point? (Check
   online and in local papers.) List possibilities.

3) As I look ahead to the day of our date, am I, or my date, likely to

- Have a lot of time and energy for the date?
- Have less time and energy (how much)?
- Have a preference for indoors or outdoors?
- Know what the weather will be?
- Know whether food will be involved (in or out)?
- Need a babysitter or have other kid issues?
- Have any transportation issues?

4) What are two dates I've led in the past that we both loved?

a)_____

b)_____

5) Can I think of a different activity other than the above two dates that inspires the same good feeling for both of us?

Remember, being on date behavior is more important than the actual activity of any given date.

Author's Note: If after wracking your brain with the above questions, the best you can come up with is dinner and a movie, make the dinner special (flowers?) and arrive at the movie early enough to have coffee and dessert beforehand, etc.

CHAPTER NINETEEN
FEEDBACK FORM

Feedback Sandwich
(A Format for Giving Feedback)

Positives (be specific):
What was effective?
What made it work?
What did you like that ___ said or did?
(name)

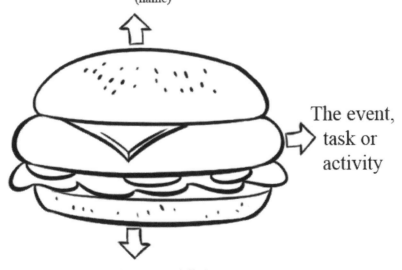

The event,
task or
activity

Suggestions (be specific):
What could have made it more efective?
What could have made it work better?
What could____ have said or done to make it more successful?
(name)

Concept by Marion O'Malley

143

Please tell us what you think, and how we could improve the TDAW plan for you!

Name:_____

Email address:_____

Mailing address:_____

(<u>Note</u>: We do *not* share lists.)

If you send us feedback, we will be happy to send you a free copy of the next edition of *Two Dates a Week*, either for yourselves or to send to a friend or family member. And you can opt to receive our free TDAW tips on our blog too. (See twodatesaweekworks.com.)

Mail this form to

TDAW

4309 Pond Rd.

Efland, NC 27243

Or go to www.twodatesaweekworks.com and click on "Feedback Form" to send it back to us electronically.

FEEDBACK FORM

"Feedback is the breakfast of champions."

Kenneth Blanchard

1. Are you in a committed relationship? For How long?

2. How long did you try the TDAW plan? How many months or dates?

3. Have both of you led dates? An equal number?

4. Results? (General or specific)

5. List the top three to five things about TDAW (the book, the CD, or the plan itself) that were most helpful for you.

6. What didn't work so well?

7. What could we do to make this plan better for you or others?

8. Any particularly great dates to report? In what city, or area of the country...or world?)**

9. Additional feedback?

10. Can we use your feedback in the following?

<u>Yes</u>   <u>No</u>

____   ____   On our website.

____   ____   In future publications.

If "yes" to either of the above two, check any of the following that are okay with you:

___ You can use my feedback, but don't identify me.

___ First name and last initial only

___ Full name is ok with me

___ City and state is ok with me

Would you like to receive *TDAW Tips* with ideas to spice up your dating life?

___ Yes

___ No

** NOTE: We're planning to follow up with 50 Great Dates in cities all over the world!

Thank you SO much for your feedback!

Go to our website: twodatesaweekworks.com

for FREE Updates and Ideas inside!

24466163R00084

Made in the USA
Charleston, SC
26 November 2013